My Father, the Captain

Jean Ferdinand Tannis

authorHOUSE®

AuthorHouse™ UK
1663 Liberty Drive
Bloomington, IN 47403 USA
www.authorhouse.co.uk
Phone: UK TFN: 0800 0148641 (Toll Free inside the UK)
*   UK Local: (02) 0369 56322 (+44 20 3695 6322 from outside the UK)*

Published by AuthorHouse 01/06/2023

ISBN: 978-1-7283-7624-0 (sc)
ISBN: 978-1-7283-7625-7 (hc)
ISBN: 978-1-7283-7623-3 (e)

Print information available on the last page.

Contents

Introduction...ix

My Father, the Captain 1
The Story of Captain Alfred George Tannis.....................7
The Day of Completion 9
The Amanda-T Was a Success...11
Tragedy Hit the Captain and His Crew 13
The Pain of Notifying the Crew's Relatives 15
The Move to Steel Hull Ships...19
My Mother, a Woman of Prayer 25
The Family 29
My Heavenly Father 31
Stories My Father Told Me 37
Captain Alfred George Tannis Had Thirteen Children 41
The Family of Isaac Tannis 43
What's in a Name? 45
Our Aunt Annette Newton-Tannis.....................................47
Our Aunt Claudine Marvell-Tannis.....................................49
Our Uncle Walter Tannis 51
A note from the author...53
Stephanie Tannis Adams...59
Uncle Philbert Tannis 61

Acknowledgements...83
Dedication 85

24 April 2022

The text of the New King James Version (NKJV) may be quoted or reprinted without prior written permission with the follow qualifications:

(1) Up to and including 1,000 verses may be quoted in printed form as long as the verses quoted to less than 50% of a complete book of the bible and make up less than 50% of the total work in which they are quoted.

(2) All NKJV quotations must confirm accurately to the NKJV text any use of the NKJV verse text must include a proper acknowledgement as follows:

Introduction

In order for younger members of this extended family to truly appreciate their *roots* and the environment from which we all came, a knowledge of the geographical territory is necessary. The Island of Saint Vincent is in the Eastern Caribbean. The nation is made up of several small islands that are known as the Grenadines. Bequia is the second largest of the islands. It is from Bequia Island that the Tannis family originated. Over the years attempts have been made at tracing the family genealogy with some success. My reason for writing this book is to leave an accurate and true history of our family from knowledge and information passed down to me from learned senior members of the nuclear family.

I want to thank God for choosing me to write this book. Although this is my first book, it was not a struggle, and because I believed in Him, my childish faith grew. It was incredible how everything came back to my memory so vividly, and looking back, regrettably so much has been left out. This book, however, is about my two Fathers of whom I love. My Heavenly Father reminded me so gentle of His ever living presence.

After the completion of *My Father, the Captain*, I threw myself back and said, "Well, I have done it." Feeling quite pleased with myself (and may I say a little pride pushed in) and as self was beginning to Exhalt itself, (oh bless the Lord) here came that still small voice: "And where I am in your book?" My readers, our God is real. He still watches over us and communicates as He did to the Patriarchs and Prophets. Knowing that I had erred, I put my hands to the heaven and asked God's forgiveness and commenced the second part of this book on my Heavenly Father. Some may not know their earthly father, but we must all be thankful that we all have a Heavenly Father. Yet so few really know Him. Knowing Him is all that matters and your life will never be the same. To the Greeks, He was the Unknown God, until the Apostle Paul made Him known to them. I am so proud that I am His child, and to have him as my Heavenly Father is the Blessed assurance of my life. When I think that God, His Son Jesus not sparing, sent him to die to bring the world back to Him, I cannot believe why so many are reluctant to know the only true God and the Only Living God, whom it pleases me to introduce as "My Father Who Art In Heaven." HE is my everything, MY King of Kings, Creator, Redeemer, Sustainer, Lover, and much, much more. He is a dependable, available Father that can be relied on. He gives me strength when I am weak, and when broken like Humpty Dumpty, He puts me together. He gives me His Presence and Peace in troubled times, and chastises me for my good. Yet He is High, lifted up, and Holy. He is my Father and yours. He is the unseen Father by all, yet through Jesus Christ died on the

Cross we can all come to Him, our sins forgiven and boldly approach His throne of Grace. There as we say, "Our Father who is in heaven," the presence of the Almighty Father is felt and in prayer. Lost in His presence, you pour out your soul to Him, thanking Him, first acknowledging His peace, goodness, tolerance, and patience. It is an amazing encounter that makes you want to talk with Him daily, even hourly. It's only when one comes to truly believe in Our Heavenly Father does one experience freedom. It is this freedom that enables me to deal with legality, unresolved for over 30 years, yet happy knowing that I am anchored safe and secure in My Father's Love.

I hope my journey with Him will be of help to you. And remember; your experiences in the valley are more valuable than those on the mountain top.

My Father, the Captain

It is with fond memories that I look back at the life of my father, Alfred George Tannis or "the Captain", as he was known throughout the Caribbean and South and Central America. Because of my father and his younger brother Isaac, the surname *Tannis* denotes vision, pride, love, and respect. I am not sure how many of my younger family members know the reason this name is so respected. As the matriarch of the Tannis family, please permit me to give a bit of background.

My paternal grandfather, Shadrach Tannis, married a lady from Barbados by the name of Flo, who eventually became my grandmother. I don't know her maiden name or very much about her. The history of my grandfather is very sketchy because he died before I was born and my father did not share much about him. However, I do remember his brother—my uncle Philbert—and will share his genealogy later.

My grandfather had five children: Claudine Tannis, Alfred George Tannis, Isaac Tannis, Walter Tannis, and Annette Tannis. (They may not be listed in the order of their birth.) All of the children at one time or other migrated to the USA; however, after several years Aunt Annette and Uncle Isaac returned to Bequia. During their stay in the USA, my father travelled to another island in the Grenadines called Union Island to study the trade of shipbuilding. Upon the completion of his training, my father, a young man from a humble and poor background, returned to Bequia with a passion and defined vision to build ships.

His first task was to build his own rowboat with paddles. Once completed, he was commissioned by others to design and build rowboats. He did this for a couple of years before building his first regulation fishing boat with sails. That was the beginning of what was to become a shipbuilding empire of this extraordinary man, who I am very proud to call my father—the Captain.

My Father, the Captain

It was at that time he met and married Elvira Rosalie, who became my mother. She was also a visionary who encouraged and nurtured my father's visions. He was encouraged to build a sloop which was named *Lady Viola* at launch, in honour of my mother, who he lovingly called Vie.

Lady Viola then became one of two sloops that transported passengers between the islands of Bequia and Kingstown, Saint Vincent. The island of Bequia depended on these two small boats. Later, other ships were added, namely *Bequia* and *Corona*, which were owned by a well-known family called McIntosh.

After a couple of years, the Captain along with his brother, Isaac (who had recently returned from the USA), decided to build a larger ship together. I imagine Uncle Isaac had the cash and the mouth and my father had the knowledge and the clout. (These are just my thoughts, not established facts.) However, due to the collaboration of the two brothers, the ship was built and named *The Esther-T,* in honour of my Uncle Isaac's eldest daughter, Esther Tannis.

On the ship's maiden voyage to Trinidad, Uncle Isaac decided he wanted to navigate the coastline and take *The Esther-T* vessel into the port of Trinidad. My father knew his brother was not sufficiently experienced for this task, and an argument led to a struggle. Uncle Isaac either fell or was thrown overboard.

This took place in a rocky, shark-infested islet of water. It is only because of the grace of God that my uncle was able to be rescued unharmed. I believe this miracle happened in order for their individual visions to be protected. When the port authority officers learned about the incident, one officer asked, "But how could that be? No one can escape that stretch of water alive."

Another officer replied, "Have you seen the man they threw overboard? He was so damn ugly even the sharks swam away from him."

This remark was the beginning of rude and cruel jokes the brothers had to put up with from others for a good portion of their lives.

At this time, the brothers were already proving to be men of destiny, and even though they went their separate ways, they were pursuing the same goals individually. Uncle Isaac continued having other shipbuilders build ships for him, while my father built his own. But my father was always available as a consultant for his brother and other shipbuilders.

One of the ships my uncle had built on the island was called *E. M. Tannis.* He also built smaller ships to go around the nearby island carrying mail, groceries, and civil servants. This was like a launch with little or no sails and powered by an engine. This ship was named *C. L. M. Tannis*, which was captained by my cousin Morris, one of my uncle's sons.

Both my father and Uncle Isaac had good ideas on ship and wealth building. All of my uncle's ships were named with the initials of his children. For example, his ship that was called *C. L. M. Tannis* was named for his sons Clive, Lennox, and Morris and his daughter Mathilda and wife, Margaret.

The ship that was called *E. M. Tannis* was named for his daughters Eilene and Esther and son Edward as well as his daughter Matilda, his wife, Margaret, and the surname, Tannis. I don't remember ships being named after his other sons, Alfred Tannis, William Tannis, Randolph Tannis, and Selwyn Tannis. But Uncle Isaac's first son, Alfred Clements Tannis, was named after my father, Alfred George Tannis. My cousin Alfred also captained *E. M. Tannis* for many years. He was an educated, loving, sociable and charismatic young man who loved his family.

Both my father and uncle were very successful businessmen. They both accumulated wealth by building ships and purchasing land and real estate. The family of Uncle Isaac Tannis remains intact to date on the island of Bequia. They are still one of the largest landowners on the island. I am extremely proud of the younger generation that carries on Uncle Isaac's legacy and heritage. To my knowledge, I am proud to say that not once has the Tannis family of either brother been accused, charged, or taken to court in litigation of any kind. Though not religious, they were honest and upright men.

The Story of Captain Alfred George Tannis

The Captain was a man of very humble beginnings, a man who rose from very little to become a multimillionaire, not only by designing and building ships, but also by owning cargo ships and acquiring plantations, land, homes, hotels, and other real estate. His vision was to own vast amounts of land and numerous sea properties but never to forget his humble beginnings. He leant out to many but borrowed only from banks.

Captain Alfred George Tannis was born on 28 October 1897. He was one of five children. He developed a vast knowledge and wisdom about both ships and wealth building. With these endeavours, one would not believe he was mainly self-taught and indisputably the best shipbuilder in the Eastern Caribbean. He built most of his wooden-hull ships single-handedly. At approximately 4 years of age, I remember seeing my father building what became our prized family ship. I also remember my cousin Hurbert Tannis and my brother Nathan Tannis going down to the ship-building site, a piece of land near the beach.

I came to realise later that the same plot of land belonged to my father's sister, my aunt, Annette Tannis. I would go to that parcel of land after school to collect curly wood shavings to play with. There would be lots of carpenter's tools used in the building trade lying around. It was not too long before I learned the individual names of all the contents of the toolbox, such as *plane*, *chisel*, *auger*, *bits*, and so on. Day after day I looked at the hull and watched as it became a big ship.

Several of the other Tannis cousins would join me for play. There was no danger playing around the ship site, and as the ship got bigger and higher, I would see my father, my cousin Hurbert, and my brother Nathan going high up on the wooden scaffolding that held up the ship as it got further and further off the ground. I would look at them as they packed oakum between the planks with heavy mallets. Even today, so many years later, I can still smell the scent of oakum. I can visualize these three hard-working men rolling the oakum as they used chisels and mallets to chink the seams in the ship. I can still remember the smell of tar as they sealed the chinks, the smell of rope, of all sizes in reels and climbing and jumping from one reel to the other. Oh, the joy it brought!

The Day of Completion

The day came when the ship was completed. The rigging was up and ready for launch. This was an amazing transformation. I remember that day from my childhood so clearly; the entire ship was painted and covered in ropes. I was about age 5 or 6.

On this amazing day, all the males of the Tannis clan came out, along with many of the males from the island, and gathered at the ship site. At the same time, the women were cooking, baking, and singing about the upcoming launch. It was a festive period. Then a man or two climbed onto the ship with a bottle of wine, strapped it to the bow of the ship, and prayed, asking God's blessing for a safe launch and continued safety for the voyages of the ship and its crew. Then they broke the bottle of wine and pronounced, "I name this ship the *Amanda T.* God bless all who sail in you."

Then men and women went on opposite sides of the ship, approximately twelve on each side, with axes. They cut down the wooden pillars that had held up the ship as it was being built. Some took hold of long pieces of lumber and others held pieces of rope that were professionally strapped to the ship for the purpose of launching.

As a Shanti woman began to sing in a loud melodious voice, "Today we Are going to launch this ship," the men and women on the ropes strapped to the ship responded by pulling and singing, "Go are we go."

The keel of the ship, which was sitting on wooden rollers made from the trunks of large trees, began to slide towards the sea. They did this for hours or sometimes days. There was so much excitement experienced during these festive moments in time, and my father supervised each launching process, making sure the keels of the ships did not slip off the rollers and land in the sand. As a child, these were unforgettable experiences—seeing the ships as they were being built and then later when they floated on the sea water. This is one of the contributions of the men who made our name, the Tannis name—one to be remembered.

The Amanda-T Was a Success

And so the *Amanda-T* ship launching was successful. Praise God! And the Captain had done it all. Thank God for this great yet humble and knowledgeable man. I now realise the knowledge, experience, and confidence required for the major task of getting a ship ready to sail.

I believe the *Amanda-T* was launched around 1937 or 1938, a few years before World War II broke out. My father was trading around all the islands. This brave and fearless man who loved the seas, the sky, and the stars was a self-taught ocean navigator. With this in mind, I would put this great man on par with Sir Walter Raleigh, Christopher Columbus, and Francis Drake. He was a man who should have been recognized for his contributions to this world, but instead has been deliberately overlooked, like other men of importance in the Bible—i.e., Joseph and Moses of Egypt—whose names were ordered to be obliterated. I would like my family to know that the Word of God says: "How can you curse those whom God has blessed?" And we are a blessed family!

A few years after World War II began, all steel hull ships were commissioned by the Crown to be used for service during the war. Realising all of the steel hull ships in the Caribbean were now in use for the Crown, a void was left in the Caribbean to transport the urgently needed oil. My father, the Captain, negotiated to make his flagship, the *Amanda T*, available to transport approximately 600 barrels of crude oil from the fields at Point-a-Pierre Trinidad to Georgetown, Demerara—now known as Guyana—for refining and returned with bags of rice and timber. From French and Dutch Guyana, he would pick up several hundred casks of red wine and other products needed during the war. From Suriname, he transported clothing and other fashionable products and materials, like perfume.

My father and his crew made two trips a month and came home every three months; however, the family was always kept informed as to their whereabouts. (Arrangements were made with agents to send a cable and wireless to the family whenever the ship sailed—e.g., sailing today for Barbados, then sailing today to Guyana.) It was during this time that my father accumulated his wealth. He travelled extensively around the Caribbean Islands, from Trinidad to Guyana, from Guyana to Suriname, Anguilla, and back to Trinidad, transporting products and materials.

After the war, my father, the Captain, increased his fleet by building another schooner named *Atlas*. Then he bought an unfinished schooner called the *Zenith*. The three ships had their own captains and crews and would trade in the same countries.

Tragedy Hit the Captain and His Crew

It was a sad day on 22 December 1951. On this day it was brought to the attention of the port authorities in Georgetown, Demerara that the *Zenith* had sprung a leak and the pumps were struggling to cope with the vast amount of water the ship was taking in. *The Zenith* had been sailing on the Essequibo River in Guyana. Sadly, my older brother Albert, who captained the *Zenith,* and several schoolboys from Barbados (whose parents had asked my father to take them on the trip around the islands) died with the entire crew during the school holidays.

Although the *Zenith* was reported to be in need of urgent assistance, nothing was apparently done by the authorities. On 6 January 1952, when my father arrived in Guyana on the *Amanda T,* the agent informed him the *Zenith* was missing. Although it seemed a hopeless case, my father hired a private plane to search the area. I can remember the pain as we received the telegram with the words I've had embedded in my heart since then: "CABLE AND WIRELESS. WE HAVE SEARCHED

LAND AND SEA AND HAVE NOT FOUND THE ZENITH AND ITS CREW."

My brother Albert was only 25 years old when he and his crew went missing. He had enough experience to be the captain of the *Zenith* or my father would not have allowed him to be the skipper. It was his third journey as captain. May all their souls rest in peace.

The Pain of Notifying the Crew's Relatives

It was with great pain and regret that my father carried out his duty of informing the relatives of the crew and the young schoolboys. That day changed the entire workings of my family and, I imagine, the families of the crew. I can still remember the pain on the faces of my parents and siblings. Our home has never been the same since that day. I can only imagine what the relatives of the crew went through. Thank God for His peace and His grace that work guard duty around our hearts.

As painful and sad as the words, "but life goes on," are, my father continued trading with his other two ships. His ships were some of the main means of transport for the area. Many people from the islands used these ships for traveling between islands, and then we had a group called "the traffickers" who transported animals and ground provisions, and also peanuts, sea-island cotton, and more. There were, of course, other such sailing ships owned by others. I do not want to disregard the many other sailing ships—some also from the island of Bequia—that did the same trading as my father. I personally believe my father's success came from him being the captain, owner, and builder with a sound vision, which in my humble opinion, made the difference.

My son Kenneth visited Bequia recently, and he reminded me of a story one of the semi-retired lawyers on the island told him. He said, "Your grandfather was a highly respected man here on the island. We shall remember him for many things, but most of all for a lesson he taught me."

Apparently, my father was at home for a couple of months on vacation. During his stay, his smaller sailing boat, called the *Transport,* had the government contract of transporting mail along with passengers, which meant the boat sailed daily Monday through Saturday. During this time another owner outfitted his passenger boat with an engine, allowing it to reach its destination of Kingstown, Saint Vincent a half hour to one hour before my father's boat. Because of that, none of the passengers wanted to travel in my father's slower mail boat anymore. Though this annoyed my father, he said nothing.

A few months later, my father, the Captain, was travelling to the mainland of Saint Vincent and decided to travel in his mail boat that morning. As he walked towards the wharf he noticed his slower mail boat was filled with passengers waiting to depart to Saint Vincent to do business because it was going to be a bank holiday weekend on the island. The fast passenger boat was docked with only its captain and crew aboard.

Some of the passengers walked for two hours from the south side of the island to catch the boat at 6 a.m.

My father asked the captain of the other boat, "What's going on?"

He replied, "My engine broke down, and we are not able to travel today."

My father walked back to his mail boat where all the passengers were so glad to see Captain Tannis and his boat captain arrive. My father looked at all the passengers and crew and said, "My friends, there are 365 days in the year, and this one is mine. I am not sailing today." With that, he turned his back to the sea and walked back to his home, leaving all of the passengers and crew amazed and dumbfounded.

He was a man of few words but great action.

The Move to Steel Hull Ships

As the world changed, my father, the Captain, expanded his vision to include steel hull ships. Doing so made him one of the first in the country to invest in that kind of ship building. In 1955 my father, along with two partners—his nephew Clive Tannis and a Mr. Stowe of Lower Bay, Bequia—bought a steel hull ship, making them the first black steel hull ship owners on the island.

The ship was being taken to Martinique for dry docking, and since I had never visited Martinique, I begged my father to take me with him. He and his two partners agreed and took my younger sister and two daughters from the Stowe family along as well. So my father, his two partners, my sister, the Stowe girls, the crew, and I departed Saint Vincent for Martinique.

Our first stop was Saint Lucia, where we had a one-night layover. The next morning as we were about to leave Castries harbor, one of the partners took to the bridge, disregarding my father's orders, and allowed himself or the second mate to take the bridge. Words were exchanged between my father and his partner. It was quite an unseemly situation and was getting worse. It reminded me of a situation that had taken place in Trinidad's Bocas, a rocky, shark-infested islet of water several years earlier. I felt sorry for my father. I realised the problems of partnership were beginning to unfold once again. I can't remember how the situation was defused, but it was. The name of that ship was the *Madanina*. I also don't remember what eventually happened to the *Madanina*—or the partnership. It was around that time that I left to study in England.

In 1970, my father's next endeavour was to purchase another steel hull ship called the *Cranbourne* or the *Cannourne*. By this time I lived in England, and in order for him to purchase this ship, my father had to come to England to inspect it and seal the purchase. I met him in Penzance, Cornwall and had the opportunity to be taken on a tour of the ship. I was so amazed at how spacious the interior of the ship was with all of its modern accommodations for the crew. My father bought the ship that day, and a few days later they left for the Caribbean. Not too long after that purchase, I'm told he bought another ship, which was much larger than the *Cranbourne*. He used this to travel between Tampa, Florida and British Honduras to trade fertiliser and timber.

The crew were all Spanish-speaking, and most of them did not like the idea of loading a ship owned by a black man. While the ship was being loaded in British Honduras, one disgruntled crew member tried to communicate his displeasure to my father, but neither understood the other's language and so the ship was loaded. However, as the ship steamed out of Port-of-Puerto Cortes, Honduras on its second voyage, the cargo that had been deliberately loaded to shift did just that, and the ship leaned and sank in the harbour of Port-of-Puerto Cortes. Because the ship sank on only its second voyage, the maritime insurer became suspicious of the claim they paid out for the loss of the ship but then decided to add a heavy premium increase on all of the remaining ships in his fleet.

My father, the Captain, was now ageing, so he turned over his estate to my brother, Hudson Kemuel Tannis, an attorney who ran all of the family businesses. My father, however, still had an appetite for the sea and a desire to add larger ships to his fleet. With that in mind, he persuaded my brother to purchase another ship that was his largest.

In 1972, the Captain came back to England to buy this large cargo ship. He contacted my family and me, and we drove to Bristol to meet him and see the ship. This was a much larger ocean liner than he'd previously had.

He was surprised when I asked him, "Don't you think it is too big?"

He replied, "No, dear, these are what is needed now in the Caribbean. If only I was fifty years younger!"

He was so excited as he showed us around the ship. He showed us the crew's accommodations. It had about twelve bunks, and everything looked so new and modern. My father was beside himself.

I said to my husband, "He reminds me of a boy who has just been given his favourite toy."

After a long visit, we said goodbye to my father. Our home was in Leicester, so we had a long drive home. Two days later, I received a panicked call from the agent at the hotel where my father had been staying.

"Is your father with you?" he asked.

After I replied that he wasn't, the agent said, "The Captain is missing. We haven't seen him for two days, and his bed hasn't been slept in. No one knows of his whereabouts. We are about to inform the police."

We returned to Bristol, worried and concerned. I asked if anyone had checked the ship.

They said, "No, do you think he may be there?"

I said, "It's the only place he knows and has access to."

As we began our search through the ship, out came my father.

I asked him, "What's going on, Pappy?" That's what I called him.

Nonchalantly, my father laughed and clapped his hands, apologising to us all with these words: "I am sorry to cause such commotion, but there is no more peaceful and comforting place as sleeping on a ship. The smell of the engine and the movement of the ship is what I need, not expensive hotels and forced conversation."

"But, Pappy, what did you eat today? "I asked.

He replied, "I can live on five loaves and two small fish."

We encouraged him to return to the hotel and not to give us such a scare again.

The ship my father bought had a Greek name that my father mentioned he did not like. He was told it would cost about 12,000 pounds to change the name and reregister the ship.

My father told me, "Those damn thieves won't make an extra penny off me. They are saying to get a new name will cost about 8,000 pounds and 2 to 4,000 more to register it."

He was getting more and more angry. The one thing my father, the Captain, hated was dishonesty. And he felt they were being dishonest with him.

Back at his hotel room, he sat silently, tapping his fingers, as he often did when angry and concentrating. He then suddenly stood up from the chair, engaged and excited.

To my husband and me, he said, "Damn it! I have just got a new name." He sat back down on the chair before quickly jumping up again, doing a little dance, and falling down with laughter on his bed, his legs moving in excitement. Then he again jumped up and kissed me, then my husband. He said, "Damn it! The name of my prize liner shall be *Alftan*," and he began laughing hysterically.

So I said, *"Alftan?"*

He said, "Yes, Yes, yes! That's the name. You haven't got it, child, you haven't got it. The name of my ship is the first three letters of *Alfred* and first three letters of *Tannis*."

We were all blown away! When my father presented the name to the agents, and they realised they had been beaten, he said, "I knew the registration of the ship was only 2,000 pounds."

This man, Captain Tan as some called him, was my genius.

My Mother, a Woman of Prayer

My mother was an intercessor and would pray fervently for her family, my father, the crew and their families, and the people of our village. I remember her singing divinely inspired hymns before and after her prayers. The words to one of her favourite hymns are,

> Brightly beams our father's mercy
> From His lighthouse evermore,
> But to us he gives the keeping
> Of the lights along the shore.
> Let the lower lights be burning;
> Send a gleam across the wave.
> Some poor fainting, struggling seaman
> You may rescue, you may save.
> Loud the angry billows roar ... (Philip Paul Bliss)

She would try to get us children to join in with her daily prayers. As I grew older, I did join my mother and learned the importance of daily, hourly prayer. She was truly a woman of God. This was seen in her compassion, care, and help she gave to all with whom she came into contact.

I remember my first Holy Communion when I was about 3. My mother taught Sunday school downstairs in our home. We sat on wooden benches made by my cousin Hurbert and my father, and after Sunday school my mother and a few of our aunties would break bread for communion. After the breaking of bread, they would divide the leftovers among the children. I can still hear my mother weeping as she sang hymns of glory and thanksgiving. Glory to God!

If I were asked to sum up my father, the Captain, without bias, I would say that he was an ambitious and unselfish man who loved his family and those who crossed his path. This was shown in his actions when he came home every three months. He did not only think of his immediate family, but also of his extended family and people of our village.

When the *Amanda T* was at home in port, my father would have the crew and other helpers bring his storage to our house: large burlap bags of groceries—100 to 200 bags of rice and beans, 15 to 20 large cotton bags of flour, several crates of salt or salted cod and smoked herrings and salted mackerels. There would be container upon container of pig snouts, tails, ears, and feet, all salted in a brine in large tins and large tins of lard oil, several 5- and 10-pound tins of butter and salt, and a butter with a deep-orange colour that the elders referred to as donkey butter. There were large drums of Rankin Biscuits, cans of condensed milk, and many more things, including sea salt grains.

Come to think of it, there was never any sugar that I can remember, but there were several unopened casks of unsweetened red wine. He also brought boxes of personal things, like clothes and toys for us, his children. Usually my father only spent three days in port before he hoisted anchor and sailed to another country. Most of the time while here at home he spent his time with the men of the island, drinking and helping them cut and sew canvases to make sails. After my father sailed, my mother would oversee the massive distribution of the items he'd brought home. She would make sure that the families, including her family in Saint Vincent, got items they needed.

I can remember as a little kid sitting on the stairs and seeing bags and bags of rice and flour being given away and thinking in my little mind, *My mother is giving away all the food*. Then when I was able to go downstairs, I noticed it was roomy again, since all of the bags were gone with just a half burlap bag of rice and some other groceries left for the family. Both of my parents were unselfish people and always aware of others in their community.

As matriarch of the Alfred George Tannis family, it's important as a born-again believer that I use this opportunity to share with the extended family and all readers the love of God and how he has guided, led, and supported me during this unexplained financial loss. I do not speak for my siblings, as I only had the privilege to discuss the subject briefly with one member and am unable to share the opinions or knowledge of any others. This portion of my book is to relate the importance of what we value most in life: our beliefs, acceptance, and trust.

Firstly I must quote the word of God, which says in Matthew 12: 25, "But Jesus knew their thoughts and said to them, 'Every Kingdom divided against itself is brought to desolation and every city or house divided against itself will not stand.'"

The Family

After the death of my father in 1981, my brother Hudson Kemuel Tannis was left as the executor of my father's total estate; however, he was killed in an airplane crash along with his son, his only legitimate child, and wife in 1986. My brother's death was not a surprise to me as the Lord had shown me in three open visions his death by accident on a plane.

I interject here the word of God in Amos 3:7: "Surely the Lord God does nothing unless he reveals his secrets to his servants the prophets." Some may ask if I am saying I am a prophet. I let my words speak for me; I say nothing.

It was apparent that no one knew anything about the family business, even though I had begged my sisters to get more involved, as I knew our brother would be killed. To complicate matters, a senior member of our family was the first to arrive in Saint Vincent. I was told this family member had arrived at our brother's chambers and asked his secretary which file cabinets belonged to Alfred Tannis Investments. The family member was given access to three filing cabinets, one of which was removed from the premises. I was told the files were handed to a lawyer of the island. It is also said further instructions were given to tenants of existing land/property that no information should be given to any members of the family. The family and extended family flew in from the USA, the UK, Canada, and other islands of the Caribbean to be met with total silence and total dismissal.

Up to the death of our senior family member, no accountability was given as to the whereabouts of the files of Alfred Tannis Investment, Ltd. To this day, no one has ever read a will nor has *any member* of Captain Alfred George Tannis's family seen any files. As far as I know, compensation for the accident of my brother and his family has never been discussed or information shared. To date, I personally cannot imagine what happened to my father's empire.

Because it is so unbelievable, each person was left to come to their own conclusion. And as Thomas Carlisle the Scottish historian wrote, and I quote "I do not believe in the collective wisdom of individual ignorance. Therefore I came to the belief, that this member gained valuable company information, which was deliberately withheld from other directors and siblings, but shared with that member's child."

But my family and readers, I don't know what happened, and I believe all of the extended family would say the same. I can live with myself and have no bitter feelings. I often say my brother's death was a tragedy, but that one family member's actions were a massacre, because that member destroyed what trust was left between the remaining siblings and other family members.

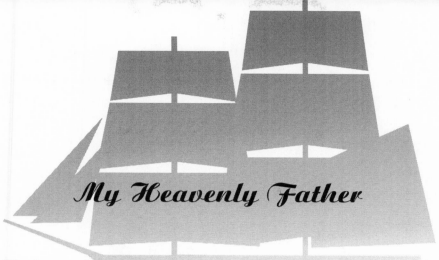

My Heavenly Father

Having read of the demise of this family, many could rightfully question how such calamity could happen.

Having written in detail, may I say as accurately as my memory allows. I now want to write of my heavenly Father, who directed the captain of the host (Joshua 5: 13–15).

Knowing Him is all that matters, for without Him we can do *nothing*. It is His love and faithfulness that keep our minds intact. What appears to the natural eye and understanding is a total loss to those of us who are born-again believers who trust in the authority and powers of our Supreme Commander-in-Chief. Our hearts remain at peace, as He instructs us. Trust in the Lord with all your heart, and lean not on your own understanding (Proverbs 3: 5).

It is our total trust in Him that brings us clarity, assurance, and peace of mind. As we cry out, "Give me, Lord, the mind of Jesus," we begin to know what He knows and receive divine revelation from His words. We are encouraged not to fret because of evildoers or be envious of the workers of iniquity (Psalm 37: 1).

During times of loss—great or small, human or otherwise—when there can be no human explanation, it is then as believers we learn to lean on He who holds the whole world in His hands. In His presence we tarry until the breakthrough comes. Bit by bit the revelation is unfolded until the entire picture can be seen and understood.

For we wrestle not against flesh and blood but against principalities, against powers, against the rulers of darkness of this age, against spiritual hosts of wickedness in the heavenly places. (Ephesians 6: 12)

God allows certain defeat in our lives to humble us and gives us the opportunity to sit at His feet, there finding sweet peace and rest. Then He gives us His assurance.

So I will restore to you the years that the swarming locust has eaten, the crawling locust, the consuming locust, the chewing locust. My great army which I sent among you. (Joel 2: 25)

For some reading, this revelation may mean nothing, but I have never doubted the word of God. I can now confidently say that the clouds are rolling back, and what *He promised* is now very visible.

Praise His Holy name. God would never allow those of His children who have clean hands and pure hearts to be defeated. He would never allow the enemy to be victorious over those who trust Him.

When we study the book of Job in the Bible, we read how God allowed what was already in Satan's heart to be fulfilled regarding Job, but God set a limit. Satan was allowed to do so much, but a holy line was drawn that Satan could not cross. Job kept on believing in the goodness of God with an understanding that He wouldn't let him down. His friends, family, and his very own *wife* did not understand. But Job knew his God and that He would end his suffering because his faith was unwavering. God gave him back that which he had lost and more.

And, my readers, guess what? God is the same yesterday, today, and forever—the *same*. Yes, He's an unbelievable God. *Yes*, no wonder the hymn writer got the vision to write:

'Tis so sweet to trust in Jesus
Just to take Him at His word
Just to lean upon His promise
Just to say thus says the Lord.

How grateful I am to have been born to a God-fearing woman who instilled the goodness of God in her children. After all is said and done, though, I stand alone. I can gladly say He has never failed me.

Satan may think he has accomplished what he set out to do, but no devil can defeat the children of God, because after Good Friday is always Easter Sunday.

∽

Most having read about the demise of the family great fortune, rightfully ask but how can such a calamity happen? I have been asked this question numerous times over the years. But I would not question the reason why.

There are times we ask God why? And there are times He gives the reason why certain things happen.

We live in a world of good and bad. Where there is evil and those who will go to any length to weaken and try to demoralize the children of God. Where there is envy, jealousy and greedy there must be vigilance and steadfast prayer. If we become weak and distracted the enemy is given an opportunity to enter and bind the Strongman and do as he pleases. But this is only for a season. Satan has NEVER defeated the children of God, and I can assure you he has not in this family either, for the very proof of this book being written shows that there are still Watchman on the walls of Jerusalem and the City is safe.

Oh! How I thank the Lord for your goodness, the Power of your Holy Spirit and your Blessed Assurance. So comforting it bring Joy to the Soul. A joy money cannot buy or replace. It reminds me of a poem I learned many years ago.

MY HOPE

I have a hope
Which never fails
When sorrow brings me low
It strengthens me
In times of Need
For I the Christ do know

Christ sorrowed too while on this Earth
While some in vigil slept
For at the death of Lazarus we are told that JESUS WEPT

Yes weeping may endure for a night but joy comes in the morning. Psalm 30:5 Do not lie there and worry in the night hours as you weep. Turn your painful sleepless night into prayer it is in these moments you build up intimacy with your God. He knows we are only human and without the help of His Holy Spirit we cannot handle our stressful situation, as children of God no longer are we burden bears. Our Jesus took all our burdens and sickness on the CROSS and once this is realized Satan has no hold on you. For you can confidently walk in the will and purpose of God for your Life knowing it doesn't matter what evil may come your way, you only have to concentrate on the Goodness and Faithfulness of God and remain on Holy Ground. At this moment I feel as if the Lord is saying to me jot a short note of encouragement and this I will do.

As one of the readers of this book you too may have had a significant loss. It may not have been monetary never the less a loss that has caused you pain and grief one you presently think you will never get over. Even as I write this loss the Holy Spirit is directing me to the loss of a loved one. A child in a tragic accident a broken marriage, broken promises. Whatever your loss do not dwell on it, there is a sure and better alternative and that alternative is Jesus Christ. It was on Him I leaned when I had no strength to stand. I leaned on His everlasting Arm, then at times I just sat in His presence and be pampered by Him. I will live over our financial loss again and again as the end result for me is "nearer my God to thee". And the same help is there for you. Do not be defeated. God is still on the throne."

Stories My Father Told Me

As I recalled these stories, I am reminded of another famous Captain, who in a hymn said, "Through many a danger Toil and snares I have already come" (Captain John Newton).

As my father began telling the stories, his eyes filled with tears, an emotion I never seen before. I call the story, "FIRE IN THE GALLEY: 600 BARRELS OF CRUDE OIL IN THE HULL." As he told the story, every word seemed to choke him as it came out. He began, "It was a rough passage. The waves were boisterous and the sea seemed angry that day. It was my watch. Broad daylight, all hands on deck. Then, I saw an unusual smoke from the galley, soon followed by the Cook. Panicking, he said, 'Captain the galley is on fire.' Immediately all hands were pulling buckets of sea water." Then, my father said a great flash flame came out the door of the galley. He said that when the realisation hit him that there were 600 Barrels of Crude Oil in the hull, a flash of Vie, my mother and the nine children came to him and he cried out with fear, "OH GOD VIE". He said suddenly a high wave splashed on the ship into the galley, and extinguished the fire. When the panic was over, the galley was covered in sand. Where the sand came from, no one understands, but he said, "I know your Mother was in prayer." He then shook his head and wiped his eyes. He said the sailors were all thankful to God, although they did not understand what happened. I say Pappy holding both his hands as they were folded on the table "That my father was the GRACE OF GOD."

The next story he told me was about how the Amanda T was anchored somewhere in Burbeice or up the Esequibo River. They were there anchored for three days, loading timber. He said he was busy supervising as usual, and on that day, he did not close his cabin door. Around mid-afternoon he thought, "I shall sit in the cabin and write the Log book." As he bent down to go in, he saw a huge snake wrapped on his bed. He quickly closed the doors and reported to the water police, who brought the right authorities to remove the snake. He said that he was told by the Captain, "You are a lucky man. This one is a CRUSHER. If you had entered in the dark, it would have been all over for you." He said that he looked to heaven and said, "Thank you Lord for I know your Mother was in prayer."

The next story has no end; I call it an Aborigines Indian and a nugget of gold. My father asked me, "Do you know what a nugget of gold looks like?" I said excitedly, "Yes!" He asked where I saw it. I said at home. I can't remember who was showing it, but many of us held it. He said, "That nugget has an interesting story but am not ready to share it today." I said,

"Come on Pappy you can't do me that." He clapped his hands and replied, "Some stories are better not told."

I thank you God for inspiring me to write this book so that all these stories and information can be shared, at times I sit in silence and think. It would have been an awful shame to have died with my family history.

TO GOD BE THE GLORY

GREAT THINGS HE HAS DONE

My father remained a very humble man, even after he accumulated his wealth and was respected by most. As far as I can remember, he never owned a wristwatch or fob watch, rings, neck chain or any other jewellery from British Guyana, as was the craze with many during that time. He rather enjoyed spending on his daughters. He bought us gold necklaces, bangles, bracelets, and earrings. We never wanted for anything.

We, the children of Captain Alfred George Tannis, may have lost our earthly inheritance, but because of our godly mother, almost all of my siblings have given their lives to Christ Jesus and now look forward to our inheritance in the New Jerusalem.

The Tannis Family Motto
"Respect and Love the Land and Sea."

Captain Alfred George Tannis Had Thirteen Children

My father had ten children by marriage, though my first brother died as an infant. I was told all the babies born that year on the island died of an outbreak of cholera. Here are the names of my remaining siblings: Inez Tannis Hazel, Albert Tannis, Hudson Kemuel Tannis, Leatrice Tannis Gibson, Pearlina Tannis Charles, Jean Lestlin Ferdinand-Tannis, Joan Creese Tannis, Keren Prescott-Tannis and Jane Amanda Francis-Tannis These are children by his marriage.

My father also had three other faithful and hardworking loyal children, for a total of thirteen. Nathan Tannis, who was my oldest brother; worked with our father and was very close to him and loved him dearly. He was my father's firstborn, a loving, loyal brother to look up too. I loved him dearly. I also have a sister called Theresa and another called Ida McCree. They all loved and respected their father.

The Family of Isaac Tannis

My uncle Isaac had eleven children—eight males and three females.

Alfred Clement Tannis, Clive Tannis, Esther Tannis, Morris Tannis, William Tannis, Mathilda Tannis, Edward Tannis, Eilene Tannis, Randolph Tannis, Selwyn Tannis, and Lennox Tannis

My uncle Isaac was a loving and caring uncle. He always paid attention to me and often bought me sweets and other treats. I can remember several occasions from when I was a teenager when he gave me twenty dollars whenever we met. He was a good family man and employer.

I believe that if my father Alfred and my uncle Isaac had reconciled and made peace with each other, the story of their contribution together to the Caribbean and Central and South America—and probably the world—would be renowned and in history books worldwide today, keeping in mind what they accomplished individually.

They obviously had a lot of charisma as both brothers courted beautiful young ladies from the mainland of Saint Vincent. My father, the Captain, courted my mother Elvira from the Windward side of the island, while my dear uncle Isaac courted Aunt Margaret, who was from the Leeward side of the island.

It is ironic that children develop their senses of self from the environments in which they grow up. Usually the family environment plays a large role in shaping the identity of children as they grow into adolescence and become adults. The way family members relate to one another and operate together as a social group can shape a child's self-esteem, socialisation, and cultural identity. It seems as if we have lost a bit of the Tannis identity over the years, especially on my father's side.

My father's family is spread out around the globe and fragmented, and we are not in touch with each other, while my Uncle Isaac's family seems to be the total opposite and has retained the Tannis unity.

The philosopher Aristotle once said, "The whole is greater than the sum of its part."

What's in a Name?

When talking about famous people, do you say *Darwin*, but *Marie Curie*? *Dickens*, but *Emily Dickinson*? Because of our male offspring, I am assured the Tannis name will continue for generations, due to the fact that the male gender keep their names while the female gender lose theirs when married, therefore giving their children their husbands' names.

On the other hand, my father's side of the family had seven female offspring. It is expected when a woman gets married that her surname will change to that of her husband, even if she decides to use a hyphenated surname. Her children are given their father's name, and her surname loses its ability for legacy—in our case, the Tannis name.

Of my father's female children, only two gave their male children the Tannis name. Hopefully the legacy of these two great men will continue for decades. Uncle Isaac has done what no other man has done on the island of Bequia by ensuring the family has its own estate with its own burial ground and chapel at his Cinnamon Garden home that includes several sustaining on-ground amenities.

This is a rare commodity and is the envy of many other families around the globe. I realise there have been and still are many great families on this island—McIntosh, Rice, Mitchel, and Gooding, to name a few. But many of these names mean very little to most on the island. But to my dear cousins and those who directly carry the Tannis name, it is important to realise the history and legacy that has been left by these two great men.

Our Aunt Annette Newton-Tannis

To complete the Tannis family of my grandfather's line, I must talk about Aunt Annette Newton-Tannis. On her return from the USA, my dear aunt Annette set out to build her house. She must have been in her forties and was a very slim, beautiful lady. She kept mostly to herself. I remember her as very hard-working. Every day she sat in the hot sun, pounding piles and piles of stone in order to build her dream home. She seemed lonely, but she was happy because she had a cause and mission and did not involve herself in anyone else's life.

Aunt Annette had four children: an older son whose name I cannot remember, Ainsley Farrel, Dorothy Newton-Morgan, and Geniveve Newton-Peters.

It seemed to have taken a long time to build, but after a while Aunt Annette's house was completed, with all of the bells and whistles of the time. It was built on the very parcel of land where the family's flagship, the *Amanda T*, was built. It was one of the few concrete houses on the island. However, not many years later Aunt Annette died. She was the first dead person I ever saw. I was still very young. She is the grandmother of Dr. Ray Morgan of Brooklyn, New York, who is the son of Dorothy Newton-Morgan.

Our Aunt Claudine Marvell-Tannis

To further complete the Tannis family of my grandfather's line I must talk about Aunt Claudine Marvell-Tannis. Aunt Claudine never returned to Bequia after leaving for the USA in her early twenties. She spent her professional life working for the US government as a registered nurse. Like her younger sister Annette, she was a very beautiful and attractive lady. She was also the historian of the family. She lived in the Bedford-Stuyvesant community in Brooklyn, New York. Aunt Claudine died in 1973 and had one child, Jean Abbott-Marvell.

Our Uncle Walter Tannis

To even further complete the Tannis family of my grandfather's line I must talk of Walter Tannis. Uncle Walter, like his sisters Claudine and Annette, migrated to the US at a very young age. I believe he returned to Bequia once or twice on very short vacations before returning to New York, where he worked on the docks as a carpenter. He, like his brothers Alfred and Isaac, invested highly in real estate, owning several brownstones in the Bedford-Stuyvesant and Brooklyn, New York, communities. Uncle Walter not only had many houses, but was also a very flashy dresser with a new Ford Thunderbird every three years. Uncle Walter was the first black man in Brooklyn to own a colour television in the 1940s. He lived in the Bedford-Stuyvesant community in Brooklyn, New York. Uncle Walter died in 1971 and had one child, Mae Clase-Tannis.

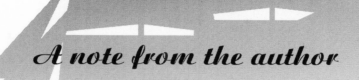

A note from the author

My name is Jean Tannis Ferdinand. I am my parents' seventh child. I was educated at the Seventh Day Adventist College in Maracas Trinidad. I have lived in the United Kingdom since 1955. I am married and have six children and many grandchildren and great-grandchildren. I have been a born-again believer since the age of 14. I worked as a registered nurse for many years as a midwife, health visitor, and district nurse.

∽

My desire is that everyone who carries the Tannis name may feel the same love that flows in my veins and that one day, on the Island of Bequia, there will be a home where family members, regardless of position or class, could book a place of quiet rest and know and feel at home. My home, your home.

Having spoken of my earthly father, the Captain, I would now like to elaborate on the goodness of my heavenly Father, who is the Captain of the Host, as without Him we can do nothing. It is He who enables us to go through the battles of life and come out uninjured.

We do not fear those who can destroyed the body, but he who can destroy both body and soul. Many questions have been asked but how such a disaster could happen it's inconceivable to the natural mind but the word of God admonish us to trust in the Lord with all our hearts leaning not on our own understanding (Proverbs 3: 5–6).

To those who are spiritual minds born again of the spirit who are led and directed by the spirit of God: Do not remain ignorant of the time and season. We are told that we wrestle not against flesh and blood, but against principalities, against powers, against the rulers of darkness of this age, and against spiritual hosts of wickedness in the heavenly places (Ephesians 6: 1).

It is my prayer and hope that the history of this family will draw each of us closer together as I use the prayer of Saint Frances of Assissi.

> Lord, make me an instrument of Thy peace.
> Where there is hatred, let me sow love; where

there is injury, pardon; where there is doubt, faith; where there is despair, hope; where there is darkness, light; where there is sadness, joy. O Divine Master, grant that I may not so much seek to be consoled, as to console; to be understood, as to understand; to be loved, as to love. For it is in giving that we receive, it is in pardoning that we are pardoned; it is in dying that we are born to eternal life.

My hope and desire is that reading this book will ignite a passion in the extended family to trace their roots, and one day the education department may use this book to teach the history of shipbuilding that was once the industry of the island—and not only on the island of Bequia, but many other islands in the Grenadines, and still is on the island of Cariacou. Though it's now, sadly, a dying industry, it should be revived.

Those of us who have lived during these times take with us such joyful and exciting memories of the Islands and our wonderful and fearless seamen who travelled daily and a group without whom the economy of the islands would not have grown. It is to these ancient mariners we owe a debt of eternal respect. And to all the families who were once part of this elite group of mariners, I give my deepest respect. To those who lost their lives at sea, we will remember thee.

In concluding my book I felt compelled to address the Tannis family as a whole. I want you, my family, to know that we are blessed. It's important that each member who carries the name and knows how to spell it correctly knows that he or she is blessed. This blessing has been handed down by God himself to our forefathers, and that blessing, my family, is the gift of wealth building. Male and female alike are blessed with this gift. All one has to do is first *believe* and *trust God*. Now that this has been revealed to you, begin to prove to yourself it is true. Share with others, and never feel tempted to be boastful or be inclined to dismiss the less fortunate.

God bless you all.

My dear citizens of Bequia,

Although the shipbuilding trade has died, please do not let the loving community spirit die. We all need each other, and one man is not an island. I would love to know the sweet memories of my childhood continue despite all modern developments and technologies.

How we all worked together in unity! One of my favourite memories is how as children we learned our twelve times table. Only a few of us are alive to reminisce about how, as little ones on foot, we started from Hamilton stopping at each entrance to collect one another for school.

The older pupils started the Shanti song:
"Twice one are two."

And we the younger ones repeat:
"Twice one are two."
The older ones continue:
"Twice two are four."
And the younger repeat.
Then the older say, "Twice three are six" and "Twice four are eight."

And we are singing and running until we get to school. When one reaches the age of 8 or 9, we all know our twelve times table by heart. No computers, no calculators, but just loving neighbourhood spirit. I pray that the spirit remains with all, especially those who are indigenous to this wonderful island Bequia.

Also, I hope that sometime soon the government will consider the area of Hamilton for building and development. There has been <u>deliberate political neglect</u>. The area should be seen as a place of historical interest. Hamilton may not be a tourist attraction; however, it is a valuable part of Bequia.

You may ask how I could survive such painful loss during this period of adversity.

I recommend every reader do what I do and daily remind themselves of this hymn sung be the Mississippi Mass Choir: "Your Grace and Mercy Brought Me Through." Invest in this album, and play it over and over until you realise that although disappointment is unavoidable, discouragement is a choice.

Stephanie Tannis Adams

the Matriarch of the Philbert Tannis family

(born 1934)

It was a pleasure working with a knowledgeable member of our family who has such zeal but who is, more importantly, a prayer warrior. Her son Roseman Adams was passionate and informative and pleased to have passed on to me the work he had completed on the family tree. He is a family member to whom all the family should show their gratitude. Again, to both of you, I say *thank you* for your contributions.

Uncle Philbert Tannis
(born 1869)

As a child, I remember thinking of Uncle Philbert as a very elegant and tall man who walked upright, even at an advanced age. I was fascinated by him because he was the grandpa I never had. All my cousins in the village felt the same way about him.

Uncle Philbert had several children. Some I may remember inaccurately, so forgive me if I am in error with the names. Uncle Philbert's children include: Hurbert Tannis, Conrad Tannis, Vincent Tannis, Bosie Tannis, John Tannis, Gurtrude Tannis, Lucy Tannis, Malita Tannis, and Lydia Tannis.

As a village, we worked, played, and shared almost everything. But as small children we played more with our cousins, mostly Uncle Hurbert's children, Stephen, Stephanie, and James. Hurbert Tannis is the grandfather of Patrick Tannis.

So, as you can see, my dear family, we are all one.

Jean Ferdinand Tannis

 ancestry

Tannis

2nd great-grandfather

Facts

Family

Parents

Spouse & Children

 Sheddie Tannis

Philbert Tannis

Sources

ancestry

Philbert Tannis

BIRTH Unknown
DEATH Hamilton , Bequia, Grenadines, St Vincent and the Grenadines
great-grandfather

Facts

Birth of Son Herbert Tannis (1905–1979)
19 Feb 1905

Death of Son Herbert Tannis (1905–1979)
19 May 1979 • Port Elizabeth, Grenadines, St Vincent and the Grenadines

Death
Hamilton , Bequia, Grenadines, St Vincent and the Grenadines

Family

Parents

👤 Tannis

Spouse & Children

👤 Suzannah Burgin

   👤 Lucy Tannis

   👤 Malita Tannis

   👤 Madgerie Tannis

   👤 Lydia Tannis

   👤 Philomena Tannis

   👤 George Tannis

   👤 Vincent Tannis

   👤 John "Boyie" Tannis

Spouse & Children

   👤 Herbert Tannis
      1905–1979

Sources

Philomena Tannis

BIRTH Trinidad and Tobago
DEATH Unknown
grandaunt

Facts

Age 0 — **Birth**
Trinidad and Tobago

Birth of Half-Brother Herbert Tannis (1905–1979)
19 Feb 1905

Death of Half-Brother Herbert Tannis (1905–1979)
19 May 1979 • Port Elizabeth, Grenadines, St Vincent and the
Grenadines

Family

Parents

Philbert Tannis

Suzannah Burgin

Spouse & Children

Enid Tannis

Conrad Tannis

Sources

Madgerie Tannis

grandaunt

Facts

Birth of Half-Brother Herbert Tannis (1905–1979)
19 Feb 1905

Death of Half-Brother Herbert Tannis (1905–1979)
19 May 1979 • Port Elizabeth, Grenadines, St Vincent and the Grenadines

Family

Parents

👤 **Philbert Tannis**

👤 **Suzannah Burgin**

Spouse & Children

👤 **Lawerence Quashie**

   👤 **Micheal Quashie**

   👤 **Octavia Quashie**

   👤 **Allison Quashie**

   👤 **Fred Quashie**

   👤 **Stacy Quashie**

   👤 **Hulda Quashie**

   👤 **Isoline Quashie**

Sources

ancestry

Lydia Tannis

BIRTH Bequia , Grenadines, St Vincent and the Grenadines
DEATH Unknown
grandaunt

Facts

Age 0 — **Birth**
Bequia , Grenadines, St Vincent and the Grenadines

Birth of Half-Brother Herbert Tannis (1905–1979)
19 Feb 1905

Death of Half-Brother Herbert Tannis (1905–1979)
19 May 1979 • Port Elizabeth, Grenadines, St Vincent and the Grenadines

Family

Parents

Philbert Tannis

Suzannah Burgin

Spouse & Children

Eurnice Lewis

Telena Lewis

Vinda Lewis-Simmons

Sources

1/1

Lucy Tannis
grandaunt

Facts

Birth of Half-Brother Herbert Tannis (1905–1979)
19 Feb 1905

Death of Half-Brother Herbert Tannis (1905–1979)
19 May 1979 · Port Elizabeth, Grenadines, St Vincent and the Grenadines

Family

Parents

- Philbert Tannis
- Suzannah Burgin

Spouse & Children

- Joseph Burgin
  - Christobel Burgin
  - Maxi Burgin

Spouse & Children

- Exekiel Gregg
  - Leannie Gregg
  - Lutina Gregg
  - Louis Gregg
  - Seaton Gregg

Sources

7/3/2021   Ancestry Person - Print

ancestry

John "Boyie" Tannis
granduncle

Facts

Birth of Half-Brother Herbert Tannis (1905–1979)
19 Feb 1905

Death of Half-Brother Herbert Tannis (1905–1979)
19 May 1979 • Port Elizabeth, Grenadines, St Vincent and the
Grenadines

Family

Parents

👤 **Philbert Tannis**

👤 **Suzannah Burgin**

Spouse & Children

👤 **Grace Chambers**

👤 **Cassian Tannis**

👤 **Janice Tannis**

👤 **Genieva Tannis**

👤 **Authon Tannis**

👤 **Allington Tannis**

👤 **Moretta Tannis**

👤 **Julie Tannis**

Spouse & Children

👤 **Theresa Tannis**

👤 **Teckla Tannis**

👤 **Dawn Tannis**

👤 **Regina Tannis**

Sources

https://www.ancestry.com/family-tree/person/tree/83512701/person/412283405728/facts   1/1

James Tannis
uncle

Facts

Birth of Sister Stephanie Eloise Tannis (1934–)
23 12 1934 • Hamilton, Bequia, St. Vincent and the Grenadines

Death of Father Herbert Tannis (1905–1979)
19 May 1979 • Port Elizabeth, Grenadines, St Vincent and the Grenadines

Death of Mother Irene Quashie (1909–1991)
/ 11/ 1991 • Kingstown, Saint George, St Vincent and the Grenadines

Family

Parents

 Herbert Tannis
1905–1979

 Irene Quashie
1909–1991

Spouse & Children

 Sylvester Tannis

Sources

⇥ancestry

Herbert Tannis

BIRTH 19 FEB 1905
DEATH 19 MAY 1979 • Port Elizabeth, Grenadines, St Vincent and the Grenadines
maternal grandfather

Facts

Age 0 — **Birth**
19 Feb 1905

Age 29 — **Birth of Daughter Stephanie Eloise Tannis** (1934–)
23 12 1934 • Hamilton, Bequia, St. Vincent and the Grenadines

Age 74 — **Death**
19 May 1979 • Port Elizabeth, Grenadines, St Vincent and the Grenadines

Family

Parents

👤 **Philbert Tannis**

Spouse & Children

👤 **Ruth Harris**

👤 **Cora Harris Tannis**

Spouse & Children

👤 **Irene Quashie**
1909–1991

🖼 **Stephanie Eloise Tannis**
1934–

👤 **David Tannis**

👤 **Edson Milton Tannis**

👤 **Jenny Tannis**

👤 **Bernice Tannis**

👤 **Syble Tannis**

👤 **James Tannis**

👤 **Steven Tannis**

👤 **Cynthia Tannis**

Sources

⫸ancestry

Diana Sherma Adams

BIRTH 29 02 1964 • Kingstown, Saint George, St Vincent and the Grenadines
DEATH Living
sister

Facts

Age 0 — **Birth**
29 02 1964 • Kingstown, Saint George, St Vincent and the
Grenadines

Age 2 — **Birth of Sister Beverly Ann Adams** (1966–)
15 11 1966 • Clifton, Union Island, St. Vincent and the
Grenadines

Age 5 — **Birth of Brother Roseman Adams** (1969–)
2 Dec 1969 • Clifton, Union Island, St. Vincent and the
Grenadines

Age 8 — **Birth of Brother Victor Ashley Fraser** (1973–)
24 02 1973 • Kingstown, Saint George, St Vincent and the
Grenadines

Age 20 — **Death of Father Benjiman Aurthur
Adams** (1930–1984)
21 05 1984 • Kingstown, Saint George, St Vincent and the
Grenadines

Age 28 — **Birth of Child Shenelle Ann-Marie
Thomas** (1992–)
22/07/1992 • London, England

Age 34 — **Birth of Son Anthony Sherwin
Thomas** (1998–)
15 12 1998 • Kingstown, Saint George, St Vincent and the
Grenadines

Family

Parents

Benjiman Aurthur Adams
1930–1984

Stephanie Eloise Tannis
1934–

Spouse & Children

Benedict Anthony Thomas

    Shenelle Ann-Marie Thomas
    1992–

    Anthony Sherwin Thomas
    1998–

Sources

Other Sources

Facebook

Cynthia Tannis
BIRTH Unknown
DEATH Living
aunt

Facts

Birth of Sister Stephanie Eloise Tannis (1934–)
23 12 1934 • Hamilton, Bequia, St. Vincent and the Grenadines

Death of Father Herbert Tannis (1905–1979)
19 May 1979 • Port Elizabeth, Grenadines, St Vincent and the Grenadines

Death of Mother Irene Quashie (1909–1991)
/ 11/ 1991 • Kingstown, Saint George, St Vincent and the Grenadines

Family

Parents

Herbert Tannis
1905–1979

Irene Quashie
1909–1991

Spouse & Children

Bertram Hope

Carlos Hope

Spouse & Children

Conrad Alexander Adams

Seymour Tannis

Spouse & Children

Annis Shirley Tannis

Deborah Tannis

Sources

ancestry

Roseman Adams

BIRTH 2 DEC 1969 • Clifton, Union Island, St. Vincent and the Grenadines
DEATH Living

Facts

Age 0 — Birth
2 Dec 1969 • Clifton, Union Island, St. Vincent and the
Grenadines

Age 3 — Birth of Brother Victor Ashley Fraser (1973–)
24 02 1973 • Kingstown, Saint George, St Vincent and the
Grenadines

**Age 14 — Death of Father Benjiman Aurthur
Adams** (1930–1984)
21 05 1984 • Kingstown, Saint George, St Vincent and the
Grenadines

**Age 34 — Birth of Daughter Ashara Rukiya Deah
Adams** (2004–)
18 11 2004 • Scarborough, Toronto, Ontario, Canada

**Age 37 — Birth of Son Akaroese Julius Benjiman
Adams** (2007–)
17 06 2007 • Scarborough, Toronto, Ontario, Canada

Family

Parents

Benjiman Aurthur Adams
1930–1984

Stephanie Eloise Tannis
1934–

Spouse & Children

Sherma Patricia Ann-marie Selby
1970–

Ashara Rukiya Deah Adams
2004–

Akaroese Julius Benjiman Adams
2007–

Sources

ancestry

Stephanie Eloise Tannis

BIRTH 23 12 1934 • Hamilton, Bequia, St. Vincent and the Grenadines
DEATH Living
mother

Facts

Age 0 — Birth
23 12 1934 • Hamilton, Bequia, St. Vincent and the Grenadines

Age 21 — Birth of Daughter Jane Cudjoe (1956–)
03 07 1956

Age 29 — Birth of Daughter Diana Sherma Adams (1964–)
29 02 1964 • Kingstown, Saint George, St Vincent and the Grenadines

Age 31 — Birth of Daughter Beverly Ann Adams (1966–)
15 11 1966 • Clifton, Union Island, St. Vincent and the Grenadines

Age 34 — Birth of Son Roseman Adams (1969–)
2 Dec 1969 • Clifton, Union Island, St. Vincent and the Grenadines

Age 38 — Birth of Son Victor Ashley Fraser (1973–)
24 02 1973 • Kingstown, Saint George, St Vincent and the Grenadines

Age 44 — Death of Father Herbert Tannis (1905–1979)
19 May 1979 • Port Elizabeth, Grenadines, St Vincent and the Grenadines

Age 49 — Death of Husband Benjiman Aurthur Adams (1930–1984)
21 05 1984 • Kingstown, Saint George, St Vincent and the Grenadines

Age 56 — Death of Mother Irene Quashie (1909–1991)
/ 11/ 1991 • Kingstown, Saint George, St Vincent and the Grenadines

Family

Parents

Herbert Tannis
1905–1979

Irene Quashie
1909–1991

Spouse & Children

Benjiman Aurthur Adams
1930–1984

Jane Cudjoe
1956–

Diana Sherma Adams
1964–

Beverly Ann Adams
1966–

Roseman Adams
1969–

Victor Ashley Fraser
1973–

Rochelle

Nikkay Rock

Samuel Gerald Adams

Kenneth Reynold Adams

Sources

⊰ancestry

Steven Tannis
uncle

Facts

Birth of Sister Stephanie Eloise Tannis (1934–)
23 12 1934 • Hamilton, Bequia, St. Vincent and the Grenadines

Death of Father Herbert Tannis (1905–1979)
19 May 1979 • Port Elizabeth, Grenadines, St Vincent and the Grenadines

Death of Mother Irene Quashie (1909–1991)
/ 11/ 1991 • Kingstown, Saint George, St Vincent and the Grenadines

Family

Parents

Herbert Tannis
1905–1979

Irene Quashie
1909–1991

Spouse & Children

Patrick Tannis

Andrew Octave

Calbert "Callie" Straker

Cuthbert Maxwell Tannis

Sources

ancestry

Sylvester Tannis
BIRTH Unknown
DEATH Living
maternal 1st cousin

Facts

Family

Parents

James Tannis

Spouse & Children

Peters

Roneisha Tannis

Spouse & Children

"Wina"

Rochelle Tannis

Racquel Tannis

Spouse & Children

Karen Tannis

Sources

Telena Lewis

1st cousin 1x removed

Facts

Family

Parents

👤 **Eurnice Lewis**

👤 **Lydia Tannis**

Spouse

👤 **O'Garro**

Spouse & Children

👤 **Conrad Phillips**

👤 **Francis Phillips**

👤 **Kemis Phillips**

👤 **Mc Karty Phillips**

👤 **Agnes Lewis**

👤 **Griar Lewis**

👤 **Casilda Lewis**

Sources

≪ancestry

Vincent Tannis
granduncle

Facts

Birth of Half-Brother Herbert Tannis (1905–1979)
19 Feb 1905

Death of Half-Brother Herbert Tannis (1905–1979)
19 May 1979 · Port Elizabeth, Grenadines, St Vincent and the
Grenadines

Family

Parents

  Philbert Tannis

  Suzannah Burgin

Spouse & Children

  Violet Frederick

    Hyacinth Tannis

    Kay Tannis

    Charmaine Tannis

    Godwyn "Brod" Tannis

    Claudette "Small" Tannis

    Winston "Big" Tannis

    Franklyn Tannis

    Mearl Tannis

    Daphne Tannis

    St. Clair Tannis

    Elton Tannis

Spouse & Children

    Maida Tannis

    Claude Tannis

Sources

ancestry

Vinda Lewis-Simmons

1st cousin 1x removed

Facts

Family

Parents

Eurnice Lewis

Lydia Tannis

Spouse & Children

Dillon Simmons

Uriel Simmons

Katehy Simmons

Gladwin Simmons

Brontie Simmons

Cornielius Simmons

Yvonne Simmons

Titus Simmons

Valorie Simmons

Terah Simmons

Yolanda Simmons

Grace Simmons

Lydia Simmons

Aswald Simmons

Valcina Simmons

Sources

ancestry

Cora Harris Tannis
BIRTH St. Vincent
DEATH Living
aunt

Facts

Age 0 — **Birth**
St. Vincent

Birth of Half-Sister Stephanie Eloise Tannis (1934–)
23 12 1934 • Hamilton, Bequia, St. Vincent and the Grenadines

Death of Father Herbert Tannis (1905–1979)
19 May 1979 • Port Elizabeth, Grenadines, St Vincent and the
Grenadines

Family

Parents

 Herbert Tannis
1905–1979

 Ruth Harris

Spouse & Children

 Clarence Tannis

 Garfield Harris

Sources

Conrad Tannis
1st cousin 1x removed

Facts

Family

Parents

Philomena Tannis

Spouse & Children

Christine Jarvis

Marva Tannis

Dennis Tannis

Philomena Tannis

Willis Tannis

Kenneth Tannis

Philmo Tannis

George Tannis

Sources

-⊁ancestry

Beverly Ann Adams

BIRTH 15 11 1966 • Clifton, Union Island, St. Vincent and the Grenadines
DEATH Living
sister

Facts

Age 0 — Birth
15 11 1966 • Clifton, Union Island, St. Vincent and the
Grenadines

Age 3 — Birth of Brother Roseman Adams (1969–)
2 Dec 1969 • Clifton, Union Island, St. Vincent and the
Grenadines

Age 6 — Birth of Brother Victor Ashley Fraser (1973–)
24 02 1973 • Kingstown, Saint George, St Vincent and the
Grenadines

**Age 17 — Death of Father Benjiman Aurthur
Adams** (1930–1984)
21 05 1984 • Kingstown, Saint George, St Vincent and the
Grenadines

Age 26 — Birth of Son Mazen Wilson (1992–)
15 12 1992 • Scarborough, Toronto, Ontario, Canada

Age 28 — Birth of Daughter Teanelle Wilson (1995–)
29 06 1995 • Scarborough, Toronto, Ontario, Canada

Family

Parents

Benjiman Aurthur Adams
1930–1984

Stephanie Eloise Tannis
1934–

Spouse & Children

Boysin Wilson

Mazen Wilson
1992–

Teanelle Wilson
1995–

Sources

Acknowledgements

To these members of the extended family who have welcomed me and shown me love and respect whenever I visited the beautiful island of Bequia.

To the late Dillon and Vinda Simmons and their daughters.

To Matilda Tannis and her brother Edward Tannis who always ensured I was made welcome and always extended the use of a private vehicle for my family when we visited. They demonstrated what family is about. I hope this will not change, though the years may change. Again, I say thank you.

To my cousin Dr. Ray Morgan. I especially want to thank him for initially proofreading my manuscript and for his other contributions.

To my young and faithful son in Christ Yannick Marie from Mauritius who encouraged me in prayer and endeavoured to find the most suitable publisher, thank you.

To my children and grandchildren who constantly reminded me to continue with the manuscript, especially my granddaughter Candice Ray-Ann Ferdinand, again I say *thank you*.

To my grandson Benjamin Ferdinand, who made technology look so easy, as he concluded all correspondence. Thank you, Big Ben.

And to Jane Jenner, a total stranger but an answer to my prayer, who helped me with technology. She is a dedicated cares coordinator for St. Ives. Thank you.

Dedication

I dedicate this book to my late father, Captain Alfred George Tannis, who was a brave and generous man. To my mother Elvira Rosalie Tannis, a woman who displayed all the qualities of Proverbs 31, and who I know was the main sail in the wind behind my late father's success.

To Uncle Isaac Tannis and his late wife Margret Tannis and their family, with special remembrance of their late firstborn son, Alfred Clements Tannis, who captained the *E. M. Tannis* for many years and who was loved and respected by all, at home and abroad.

To all my brothers and sisters all of whom have passed, save one. To my senior brother, Nathan Tannis, a hardworking, loyal, and devoted person. To my brothers Albert Tannis and Hudson Kemuel Tannis, who both died at sea under different circumstances. We will meet again someday.

To my sister Inez Hazel and her husband Ormond Hazel, a brother-in-law whose kindness, love, tolerance, and integrity will always be remembered.

To my sister Leatrice Gibson, one of the most genuine and misunderstood individuals I've known, who was a dedicated, loving family member that could always be relied on.

To my sisters Pearlina Charles, Joan Crease, and Karen Prescott, as well as to my last sister alive, Jane Amanda Tannis Francis.

There are two other sisters, Ida McCree and Thresa, who I love and respect.

I dedicate this book to my late cousin Hurbert Tannis, who worked with my father for as long as I can remember, a true and faithful family man. I also dedicate this book to my late husband Raymond Fredrick Ferdinand, who always encouraged me to write. To our five children, Keith Ferdinand, our twin daughters Sonia And Susan Ferdinand, who were born on the Island of Saint Vincent, and our son Kenneth Ferdinand. To our last child, Sarah Ferdinand. All are proud to be Vincentians.

And to my dear son Sotyne Leroy Wakama of Nigeria.

May the blessings of God continue to flow on each of them and through each of them so others' lives may be enriched.

This book is also dedicated to three men who impacted my young life one way or the other. The first is Popo Simmons. The second is Captain Reggie McCree, and the third is Jimmy Hercules.

Finally, I dedicate this book to the many young seamen that worked with my father and his brother Isaac over the years. Without these talented, skilled, and naturally born seamen, their ventures would have been limited. To all their families I say on behalf of all the Tannis family a grateful thank you.

Special Dedication

To my brother the late Hudson Kemuel Tannis whose life was cut short by that fatal plane accident that also took the life of his only legitimate child Ordway and his wife Christine Tannis. Memory of him as a father to his other children. To his work on the island a barrister at law LLB Lincoln Inn UK and as a politician for many years.

Of him it is said "H.K. Tannis went into politics a rich man but he came out poor". That of course in the eyes of most but to those of us who are believers in Christ Jesus. He came out richer than he ever was and now rest in a City not built by man's hand and a City where the Roses never fades. Praise God.

The late Hudson Kemuel Tannis was former Deputy Prime Minister and Minister of Foreign Affairs under the St. Vincent and the Grenadines Labour Party, and was on his untimely death leader of the opposition.

The Matriarch of the Shadrach-Tannis Family

Captain Alfred George Tannis with two
of his young grandsons in England, 1969.

The Matriarch of the Philbert-Tannis Family